START

FOOT   FOOT

5

FAMALLILY

CONTENTS

INTRODUCTION

The Crazier Phrazies in this book are just like the Crazy Phrazies in our first book, only ... well, a little bit stranger. Each Crazy Phrazie takes a familiar phrase, saying, title, or compound word and depicts it literally. LISTEN UP might be presented as the letters of LISTEN in a stack from the bottom up, and WORK IN PROGRESS might be PROGWORKRESS (the word WORK tucked between the PROG and RESS of PROGRESS). By using the placement or appearance of the words as clues, along with some symbols, simple drawings, and a smattering of puns, you should be able to decipher the meaning of each Crazy Phrazie. Gray lines separate puzzles on the same page. One more thing: Be on the lookout for phrases that use more than one trick. BE ON THE LOOKOUT, for example, could be shown as:

BE
LOOK

If a Phrazie should stump you along the way, you can come back to it, or you can always ANSLOOKWERS.

Sit & Solve®

Crazier Phrazies

PUZZABILITY

PUZZLE
WRIGHT
PRESS

New York

Puzzlewright Press, the distinctive Puzzlewright Press logo, and Sit & Solve
are registered trademarks of Sterling Publishing Co., Inc.

2 4 6 8 10 9 7 5 3

Published by Sterling Publishing Co., Inc.
387 Park Avenue South, New York, NY 10016
© 2011 by Puzzability
Distributed in Canada by Sterling Publishing
^{c}/o Canadian Manda Group, 165 Dufferin Street
Toronto, Ontario, Canada M6K 3H6
Distributed in the United Kingdom by GMC Distribution Services
Castle Place, 166 High Street, Lewes, East Sussex, England BN7 1XU
Distributed in Australia by Capricorn Link (Australia) Pty. Ltd.
P.O. Box 704, Windsor, NSW 2756, Australia

Sterling ISBN 978-1-4027-8263-3

For information about custom editions, special sales, premium and
corporate purchases, please contact Sterling Special Sales
Department at 800-805-5489 or specialsales@sterlingpublishing.com.

www.puzzlewright.com

MEREPEAT

PO **FISH** ND

CHEESE

tim

B l S U
p a
N e I S
s u
E r S e

WET
EAR EAR

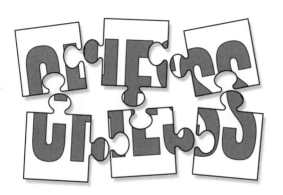

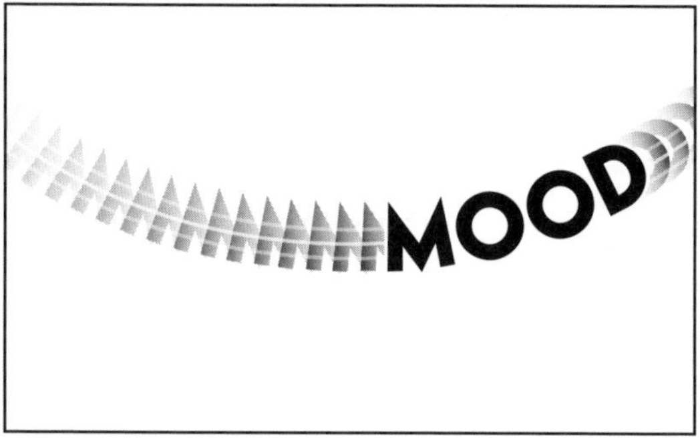
MOOD

SITTING

STILL AT

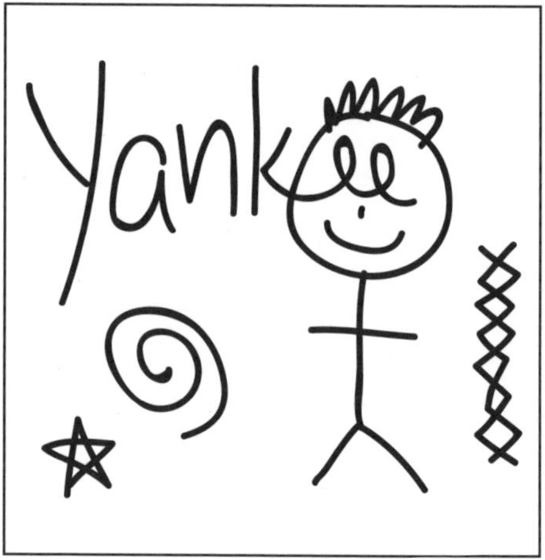
Yankee

egagtrom

I
i stnad

PE   A
SO   UP

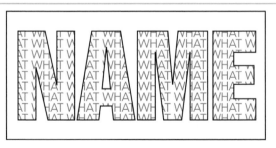

GETTING

THE MAYFLOWER

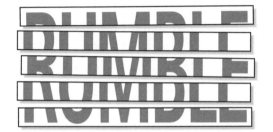

sneakers

sneakers

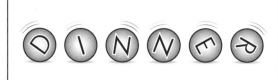

WI**TAX**TH

CHARMING

I'm home

HAIRPIN

NAVEL

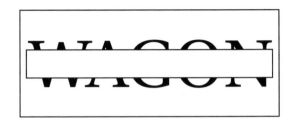

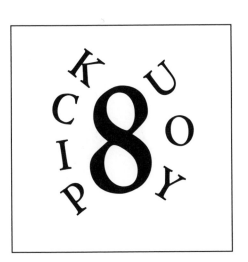

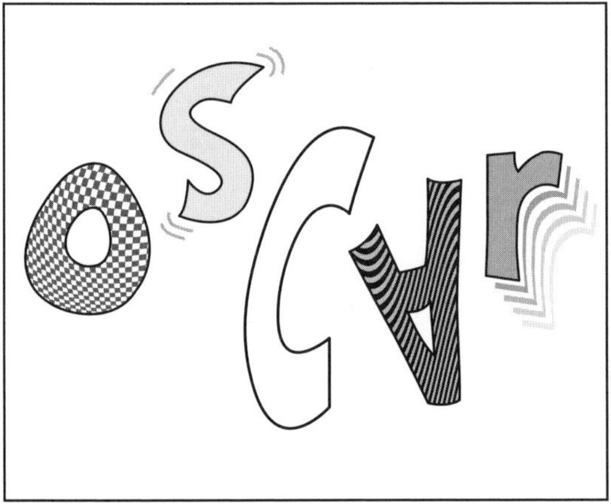

FEVER

FIVE O,CLOCK

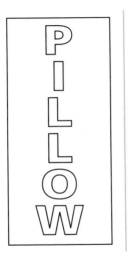

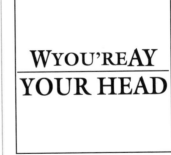

SPELL

RECEIVER

THE MORNING → YOU

AAGGEENNTT

DEADMANMANMANMANMAN

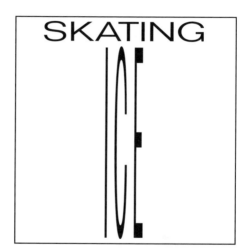

NIGHT EKAW (wake)

matrimony

When I'm

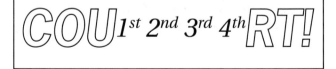

COU1st 2nd 3rd 4thRT!

Nessie
Godzilla
The Blob

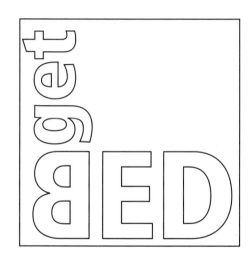

LOOKING

TURN

MY DOTTED

KRINDS

WINNER WINNER WINNER WINNER WINNER WINNER WINNER WINNER WINNER

PRESSURE
BUCKLE

NE*friend*ED = DE*friend*ED

writer

DOCTORS

FATHER

MODFIELDOM

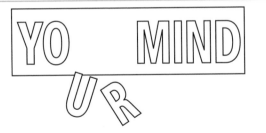

YOUR MIND

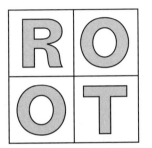

F L O R I D A

**BEEF
TOAST**

man

man man

PLCOMEACE PLACE PLACE PLACE

current

my ωεδδιπζ

COMING HOME

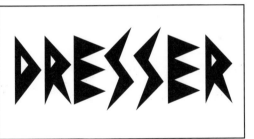

DRESSER

GRAVEYARD

PE CE

HAND

REIN

REIN

ORDER ORDER ORDER JUST

do it

6 7 1 5 2
3 8 4 9

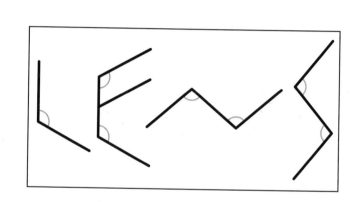

LEA **PLAYING** GUES

YOU'RE THE

blood

bbreakfasted

GETTING BAIL

CUTTING
EXPENSES

EARLT

COSTUME SSERD

WRAPPED

YOUJUSTME

$$\frac{a^4b^2 - x^3}{a^2b^3 + x} = \text{risk}$$

MOVE

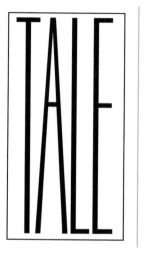

LOOK

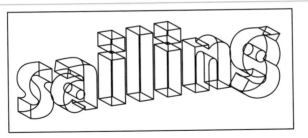

P
U
T
WRITING

ENDING
NOTE

ANSWERS | 91

5: start out on the right foot
6a: curling iron
6b: *All in the Family*
7a: musical numbers
7b: repeat after me
8: big fish in a small pond
9a: heat wave
9b: go for broke
10a: string cheese
10b: Tiny Tim
11: just in the nick of time
12: mixing business with pleasure
13a: wet behind the ears
13b: pumpkin patch
14a: square peg in a round hole
14b: Sloppy Joe
15: chess pieces

16: mood swing
17a: sitting on the sidelines
17b: still at large
18a: held in high esteem
18b: come down with a cold
19: round-robin
20: "Yankee Doodle"
21a: reverse mortgage
21b: I stand corrected
22a: split pea soup
22b: what's in a name?
23: gross income
24: getting backed into a corner
25a: The Mayflower Compact
25b: come up with a bright idea
26a: rumble strips
26b: little voice inside my head

27: high-top sneakers
28: no money down
29a: put on makeup
29b: cough drops
30a: dinner rolls
30b: pig in a poke
31: star-crossed lovers
32: balanced meal
33a: withholding tax
33b: vanishing act (or disappearing act)
34a: Prince Charming
34b: "Honey, I'm home!"
35: a twist in the plot
36: hairpin turns
37a: "Stars and Stripes Forever"
37b: fuzzy navel
38a: covered wagon

38b: three wise men
39: pick you up around eight
40: Oscar Wilde
41a: popping the question
41b: apple turnover
42a: spring fever
42b: five o'clock shadow
43a: down pillow
43b: you're in way over your head
44: fancy pants
45a: spell-checked
45b: wide receiver
46a: top of the morning to you
46b: double agent
47: dead man's curve
48: skating on thin ice
49a: wake up in the middle of the night

49b: holy matrimony
50a: when I'm old and gray
50b: "Order in the court!"
51: *Monsters, Inc.*
52: get up on the wrong side of the bed
53a: looking after the little ones
53b: no U-turn
54a: my better half
54b: mixed drinks
55: winner's circle
56: Sleepy Hollow
57a: buckle under pressure
57b: a friend in need is a friend indeed
58a: scriptwriter
58b: odds-on favorite
59a: Doctors Without Borders
59b: father figures

60a: backfield in motion
60b: you are out of your mind
61a: square root
61b: Florida Keys
62a: division of labor
62b: chipped beef on toast
63: cut out the middleman
64: Stamp Act
65a: come in first place
65b: split decision
66a: alternating current
66b: drive-thru window
67: no smoking in the house
68: *My Big Fat Greek Wedding*
69a: coming down the home stretch
69b: sharp dresser
70a: *Dirty Dancing*

ABOUT THE AUTHORS

Puzzability, which is Mike Shenk, Amy Goldstein, and Robert Leighton, has created puzzles and contests for newspapers, magazines, web sites, TV shows, ads and packaging, and other media. In addition to the original *Crazy Phrazies*, its books include *Celebrity Crosswords*, the award-winning *Bananagrams for Kids*, and *The Brainiest Insaniest Ultimate Puzzle Book*.